JESUS & STOICISM

JESUS & STOICISM

THE PARALLEL SAYINGS

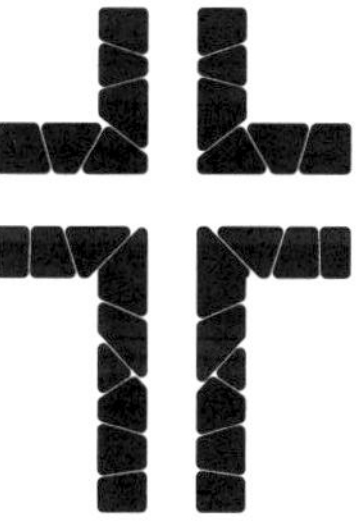

BRITTANY POLAT

Published in 2026 by
ULYSSES PRESS
an imprint of The Stable Book Group
32 Court Street, Suite 2109
Brooklyn, NY 11201
www.ulyssespress.com

ISBN: 978-1-64604-880-9
eISBN: 978-1-64604-881-6

Acquisitions editor: Claire Sielaff
Managing editor: Claire Chun
Editor: Jan Hughes
Proofreader: Sherian Brown
Creative director: Iain Morris
Interior design: Abbey Gregory
Cover artwork from shutterstock.com: grain texture © Constantin Seltea; stone cross © Ljubisa78

Printed in China
10 9 8 7 6 5 4 3 2 1

CONTENTS

AN INVITATION

Around two thousand years ago, in an outpost of the Roman Empire, a man stands before a crowd, teaching. He is dressed simply, in coarse homespun garments. He is thin from years of eating little, his beard is long, his face is weathered, but he exudes a peaceful sense of serenity, and his eyes shine brightly as he shares his message with his followers. His audience listens, enraptured, as he entreats them to turn away from the temptations of the world, to care for the people who do them wrong, and to show justice and compassion even to the downtrodden. Despite being persecuted by the authorities and forced into exile throughout his life, he is revered by the people for his personal integrity, universal love for humanity, and spiritual guidance.

His name is Gaius Musonius Rufus, and he is the leading Stoic philosopher of his day.

You are probably already familiar with another wisdom tradition born in the same region around the same time—based on the life and divinity of Jesus of Nazareth—that calls its followers to love their enemies and show charity to the poor. Jesus, of course, is well known for his teachings of love, redemption, and healing. But you might not know that Christianity was not the first ethical system of its time and place to espouse an ethos of compassion, forgiveness, and social harmony. That honor belongs to Stoicism, a philosophy and way of life that had been flourishing for around three hundred years when Jesus walked the earth.

In this book, we will examine the extraordinary parallels in the ethical systems developed by Jesus and the Stoics. Together, these two ethical systems have influenced Western ideals at a fundamental level for two millennia, inspiring individuals to lead better lives and encouraging justice on a societal scale. For these historical reasons alone, it would be worth reading texts of Jesus and the Stoics side by side. However, the goal of this comparison is not academic but rather inspirational. By studying these two venerable traditions side by side, we can see established truths with new clarity, perhaps even detecting an underlying pattern within Western ethics that points us toward a deeper understanding of ourselves and our lives.

The larger purpose of this book is to provide insight and guidance for those of us who turn to Stoicism, Christianity, or both as sources of wisdom and inspiration. In this way, *Jesus and Stoicism* follows in the footsteps of

Marcus Borg's open-hearted vision in *Jesus and Buddha: The Parallel Texts*. As a scholar of the historical Jesus and a non-exclusivist Christian pastor, Borg found deep meaning in meditating on the parallels between two great spiritual paths. He found that when we drop our need to defend whether one version is "right," we can become attuned to what is right in *both* of these traditions. As he put it, "Acceptance of religious pluralism need not generate skepticism, but can provide grounds for saying, 'Here is something I must not ignore.'"[1] In other words, when two wisdom traditions are saying the same thing, we need to sit up and pay close attention.

In much the same way, we will look at the parallels between Christianity and Stoicism, seeing where they point to a similar *way of being* in the world. That's not to say there are no differences between the two traditions—there obviously are—but perhaps because of these differences, the similarities are even more striking. While Stoicism is based in human rationality and Christianity is based on divine revelation, the fact that the two arrive at such similar conclusions surely says something very significant about the human experience.

Indeed, the differences matter too, and I don't mean to suggest that we paper over any of the substantial metaphysical or theological disagreements between Christianity and Stoicism. However, those will not be the focus of this work. Differences already receive far too much attention in our argumentative world, as so many people are eager to dispute with others and point out why they themselves are right and everyone else is wrong, or why their chosen path is better than everyone else's. This book, therefore, takes the rarer and more contrarian approach of pointing out how—despite their differences—these two ancient wisdom traditions are also very much alike. Because these similarities are most evident in the realm of ethics, we will focus most of our attention on ethical principles.

I am happy to say that I am not the first person to write about the overlapping ethical doctrines of Stoicism and Christianity—far from it. In fact, the exercise of comparing Stoicism and Christianity is as old as Christianity itself. At the time Christianity was being written down and promoted by early church authors, Stoicism was the leading philosophy throughout the Mediterranean world. Some theologians suggest that the Gospel authors Matthew and John took on board Stoic ideas, such as the ideal of ethical perfection, in writing about Jesus as Christ. The apostle Paul was very likely influenced by Stoicism in his ethical writings to the early Christian communities. One scholar goes so far as to call certain passages in Romans and Corinthians "Paul's Christian Stoicism."[2]

When we read the New Testament, therefore, it is possible that we are reading bits and pieces of Stoic ethics that were translated into early Christianity. That's not to say that Jesus himself was influenced by Stoicism or Greco-Roman philosophy; rather, the educated followers who wrote down his words and built up the early Christian community were doing so in a world where Stoicism was the dominant intellectual force.[3] They would have needed to engage with Stoic ideas at some level, even while focusing primarily on Jesus and worshiping within the Judaic tradition.

Throughout late antiquity and the early medieval period, Christian intellectuals continued to draw many ideas from Stoic thought. Classics scholar A. A. Long notes that "formative Christian thinkers, especially the Alexandrian [theologians] Clement (c. 150–220) and Origen (c. 185–254), appropriated much of [Stoicism], particularly in the field of ethics."[4] By the fourth century AD, Christianity was ascendant and the tables were turned—now the older Stoic writings had to be pleasing to Christians in order to be intellectually and ethically acceptable. Stoics such as Musonius, Epictetus, and Seneca were respected as "virtuous pagans," and manuscripts containing their works were copied and housed in monastic libraries. Epictetus, through his wise sayings in the *Handbook*, had an outsize influence on the development of Christian monastic tradition. And as scholar and theologian Elizabeth Agnew Cochran notes:

> Some Latin patristic authors found clear points of contact between Stoicism and Christianity, for example by identifying Seneca as a "sage," by speculating that the Stoics must have acquired their wisdom from the scriptures, and, in the fourth century, by forging correspondence between Seneca and St. Paul. At times, Latin authors accepted specific Stoic claims but worked to "Christianize" them or use them as "constructive tools for the formulation and defense of Christian doctrine."[5]

Quite a few of the most significant Christian thinkers of the past—Augustine, Dante, Erasmus—interacted with the Stoics in some form. However, ancient and medieval Christians were also wary of some aspects of Stoicism, particularly the Stoic defense of suicide and what they perceived as unacceptable fatalism on the part of the Stoics. And while some Stoic writings (primarily those of Seneca) remained in circulation throughout the Middle Ages, the influence of Stoicism waned until its "rediscovery" in the Renaissance, where it would covertly but decisively influence European philosophy and politics for the next few centuries.

In the early modern period, Stoicism stealthily regained prominence in Christian thought and culture. Theologians such as Martin Luther and John Calvin studied Stoic texts, many moral philosophers incorporated Stoic thought into their ethical treatises, and Stoic ideas on natural law even found their way into political systems and legal codes. And as Cochran suggests in *Protestant Virtue and Stoic Ethics*,[6] contemporary Christians can still gain much from a dialogue with ancient Stoicism. While differences are at times prominent, the points of contact between these two traditions are many and fruitful. In *The Porch and The Cross: Ancient Stoic Wisdom for Modern Christian Living*, practicing Stoic and Christian Kevin Vost points out that "we in the West are the blessed and fortunate inheritors of profoundly intertwined Judeo-Christian and Greco-Roman traditions."[7] We are fortunate indeed to have two such rich sources of wisdom.

Despite their similarities, though, you might still be asking: Can we really compare a religion to a philosophy? They might have similar ethical ideas, but aren't we looking at two totally different things? My response is: Yes and no—it's a complex question. While religion and philosophy do have some differences, they also have the potential to cover much of the same ground. Philosophy in the ancient world was a way of life that incorporated beliefs, behavior, values, and actions. It coupled the search for ultimate truth with a proto-scientific understanding of the universe, linking the underlying patterns in nature to the meaning of human life. Stoic philosophy, in particular, included a deep reverence for divinity, and piety was one of the virtues of a Stoic sage. In all of these ways, Stoicism is very similar to what we might today think of as a religion.

In other ways, though, Stoic philosophy is quite distinct from religious practice or religious experience. Somewhat confusingly for modern readers, while Roman Stoics like Marcus Aurelius and Epictetus frequently mention *God* or *the gods*, Stoic virtue is not based on theology in the same way that Christianity is. Christian ethics—insofar as it is possible to speak of the many varieties of Christian ethics under one umbrella term—derives its authority from the Bible and the divinity of Christ. In other words, it is based on faith and revelation.

Stoic ethics, in contrast, derives its authority from an appeal to human reason, with arguments standing or falling on their own merit. Although most ancient Stoics did "believe in" a type of divine power, theology has always been a *complement to* rather than *basis for*

Stoic ethics.* This enables some people to practice Stoic ethics while maintaining their commitment to a traditional religion (Christianity, Islam, Judaism, etc.). And it enables others to practice Stoicism like Epictetus and Marcus Aurelius—by trusting in a providentially ordered cosmos filled with the divine essence. Still others practice Stoicism without "believing in" any of these. In general, Stoics are happy to welcome anyone who seeks to live a better life through reason and virtue.

For these reasons, our focus in this book will be on down-to-earth concerns of ethical action rather than on theological or metaphysical aspects of Stoicism and Christianity. Contemporary Christians are invited, as Christians have done throughout the ages, to find their own way of fruitfully engaging with Stoicism and Stoic

* This point is important because it allows us to separate Stoic theology from Stoic ethics in a way very different from Christianity. Ancient Stoic theology complements ethics by engendering within us an attitude of reverence and gratitude, helping us to contextualize our human life within the greater scope of the cosmos. There are also some contemporary Stoics who follow Epictetus and Marcus Aurelius in seeing the providential patterning of the universe as a model for human life. However, if we were to remove these specific beliefs—as many modern-day Stoics have—we would still have an intact Stoic ethics. This is because Stoic ethics is independently derived through reason and observation, not based on any theological suppositions. In this way, it is quite different from Christian ethics, which is usually seen as dependent on faith. For more information see chapter 3 of Christopher Gill, *Learning to Live Naturally: Stoic Ethics and Its Modern Significance* (Oxford University Press, 2022); Julia Annas, "Ethics in Stoic Philosophy," *Phronesis* 52, no. 1 (2007): 58–87; chapter 3 of Christopher Gill and Brittany Polat, *Stoic Ethics: The Basics* (Routledge, 2024).

ethics. Practicing Stoics, in their turn, are invited to reflect on those aspects of Christianity that have contributed to its longevity and widespread appeal—for example, its emphasis on nonintellectual human capacities that speak directly to emotional experience, or its engagement with the community through works of charity.

It is in this spirit of cooperative inquiry that we explore the parallels between the words of Jesus and the Stoics. Both traditions get at the heart of what it means to be a human being who loves, seeks, wonders, and struggles; in their own ways, both these traditions embody the best of human nature, our quest for intellectual and spiritual understanding, and our perennial efforts to make sense of our experience as fallible mortals. I will echo Marcus Borg's advice to readers of *Jesus and Buddha*:

> The primary purpose of the parallels collected in this volume is not to make a scholarly case for similarity . . . Rather, the purpose of this collection is to provide opportunity for reflection and meditation. Readers will find it useful to ask a number of questions about each parallel. How are they similar? How are they different? And sometimes, by viewing the parallels together, one may have the experience

of seeing something new in a familiar saying. The sayings can illuminate each other.[8]

An open-hearted and open-minded search into the parallels between Christianity and Stoicism can yield unexpected insights into our path and purpose as humans here on earth—insights that may not be achieved by studying just one tradition on its own. So, whether you consider yourself a Christian, a Stoic, both, or neither, I invite you to ask questions, reflect on the parallel texts, ponder the shared wisdom of these two great traditions, and allow their meaning to sink deep into your heart and mind. You might find, as Marcus Borg says, that the sayings can illuminate each other—and light the way to deeper wisdom in your life.

Then he called the crowd to him along with his disciples and said: "Whoever wants to be my disciple must deny themselves and take up their cross and follow me."

—SAID OF JESUS (MARK 8.34)

This man adopts a new philosophy. He teaches to go hungry: yet he gets disciples.

—SAID OF ZENO, THE FOUNDER OF STOICISM (DIOGENES LAERTIUS, *LIVES OF EMINENT PHILOSOPHERS*, 7.27)

TWO GREAT TRADITIONS

Christianity and Stoicism, in their original forms, are both countercultural ways of life. Jesus, though steeped in ancient Jewish tradition, was a path-breaking social prophet who rebelled against the strict protocols of Judaism and what he saw as the hypocrisy of Jewish leaders. Zeno of Citium, the founder of Stoicism, created a philosophical school that rejected mainstream Greek social expectations, which were overly focused on material wealth and social position. Both of these founders inherited established and revered traditions—Jesus that of Judaism, Zeno that of Greek philosophy in the Socratic paradigm—and created their own anti-establishment versions that prioritized authenticity over exterior appearances. They rejected superficial social conventions that did not actually help people. Instead, they insisted that true abundance lay in cultivating a disposition of goodwill toward others, a willingness to make personal sacrifices, and the effort to establish a new sort of society based on virtue or righteousness.

Of course, there are differences in the contexts and cultures in which these two traditions were founded. Jesus's mission was primarily to the poor and uneducated in the countryside; we are told often throughout the Gospels that the people loved him, and this is what prevented the authorities from arresting him sooner. Not only did he have to contend with the disgruntled leaders of his own community, but he had to deal with the local Roman authorities, who eventually executed him. Religious historian Elaine Pagels suggests that they did so not at the request of the Jewish Council (Sanhedrin), as reported in the Gospels, but because the Roman governor, Pontius Pilate, perceived him as a legitimate threat to the social order.[9] Jesus was so revolutionary that all the powers that be felt threatened by him.

Meanwhile, Stoicism was born under very different circumstances. When it was founded in Athens in 300 BC (around 300 years before the birth of Christ), Greece was still the leading cultural and intellectual center of the Mediterranean region. Philosophy was a revered tradition in the Greek world, although it enjoyed what we might call a love-hate relationship with Greek society more broadly. Philosophers routinely criticized Greek society, and in turn, Greek society routinely criticized philosophers. Poets, playwrights, and statesmen both respected and were annoyed by philosophy, poking fun at the quirks of leading philosophers but also celebrating their insights. At times, the annoyance turned deadly: Socrates, the father of Western philosophy, was executed in 399 BC for daring to question and provoke the leading citizens of Athens.

Later, when Rome came to power in the region, the Romans took over the Greek philosophical tradition, including its love-hate relationship with the wider society. Stoic philosophers continued to criticize the decadence of the Roman elite, and for this, they were punished. Gaius Musonius Rufus, who was active in the first century AD (shortly after the death of Jesus), was banished from Rome by the emperors Nero and Vespasian for opposing their tyranny. Lucius Annaeus Seneca, who acted as tutor and regent to the young Nero during the early years of his reign, was later ordered to commit suicide when their relationship turned sour. (Nero obligingly sent several soldiers to Seneca's home to make sure the "suicide" was completed.) Epictetus, a student of Musonius Rufus and later one of the most influential Stoic teachers of all time, was born into slavery and witnessed both personal cruelty (his master reputedly broke his leg, causing him to limp for the rest of his life) and political chicanery at the emperor's court. Clearly, then, in ancient Rome, philosophy and politics were both dangerous professions, and the two often intertwined.

In much the same way, Jesus skillfully blended ethical teaching with sociopolitical action. His moral positions—love your enemy, help the poor, don't think you're better than other people—were aimed at both individual followers and at society more broadly, particularly at political leaders and prominent groups within the Jewish community. In all places and all times, ideas like these can get you killed, since people in power seldom like to be criticized or challenged. And yet this is exactly what both Jesus and the Stoics attempted to do, over and over again—even when a Stoic became the most powerful man in the world.

As both a committed Stoic and emperor of Rome from 168 to 180 AD, Marcus Aurelius was perhaps as close as we'll ever come to a philosopher-king. But even as Roman emperor, Marcus couldn't change the world. He came face to face with the intractable challenges of life: war, plague, death, loss, illness, betrayal, and the insatiable desire of some humans for power and wealth. Though he attempted to live as virtuously as possible, to implement enlightened policies, and to rule with benevolence and wisdom, Marcus was surrounded by petty-minded and power-hungry courtiers, treasonous lieutenants, and rebellious tribes. Not even a Roman emperor could stay the hand of greed and gluttony that afflicted Roman society.

This is, in fact, what religious and philosophical leaders have battled since the beginning of civilization: the ever-present menace of selfishness within human nature. Humans are complex and intelligent creatures who have the capacity to bring both great good and great harm to the world. Will we choose to align ourselves with the best within us—the prosocial instincts that urge us to love, to cooperate, perhaps even to forgive those who do us wrong—or will we choose to align ourselves with the false promise of external gain at the expense of other people? Jesus and the Stoics proposed different explanations for this difficulty,* but they agreed that this problem is central to human existence.

Regardless of the era or culture, all societies have needed sages and prophets to restore justice, to teach humility to those in power, to repair the ruptured relationship between humans and the world around them. Without the check of moral principles, the rich and

* The Stoics suggested that people were misled by the false teachings transmitted to them by society, as well as the inherently deceptive nature of their own impressions; Jesus wrestled the demons of temptation, falsehood, and vice, which he warned would try to deceive his followers and lead them into sin. Stoics and Christians also see different paths to salvation: for the Stoics, reason will guide us toward the blessed life, while Christians rely on divine Grace. All these sages agree, however, that truth and goodness will light the path toward enduring righteousness and virtue.

mighty will always be tempted to worship the false gods of wealth and social dominance. And in times of plenty, including our own era in the twenty-first century, this warning extends to all of us surrounded by material abundance. The allure of money and social status will always be with us. We will always need Jesus and the Stoics to remind us how to live a true and upright human life.

Both Jesus and the Stoics, in their different ways, taught us the path to a better way of being: how to overcome the ills of the world, how to keep going through loss and adversity, how to become a better brother, sister, neighbor, friend. These are the lessons these teachers have been sharing now for two millennia. The people who have picked up their mantle and sallied forth in their names haven't always done so in the proper spirit and have at times even done great harm. But whenever we return to the core of their teachings, we can see that Jesus, Zeno, Musonius, Marcus Aurelius, and their fellows have always aimed at compassion, overcoming the ego, and acting for the greater good rather than for the narrow self. They have inspired generations to love, forgive, and behave more ethically, even when no one is watching. They are unsurpassed teachers of moral wisdom.

Some people might find it strange that in this book, we are referring to Jesus and the Stoics collectively. There are, after all, some significant differences in their teachings, including different conceptions of divinity and opposing beliefs about the afterlife. But on the other hand, there are also substantial areas of overlap: many ethical parallels, including universal love and non-retaliation; an emphasis on inner qualities and internal riches; and encouragement to find and follow the proper path in life. If you like, you might think of a Venn diagram of Christianity and Stoicism, with their shared ideas represented by the shaded portion where the two circles overlap:

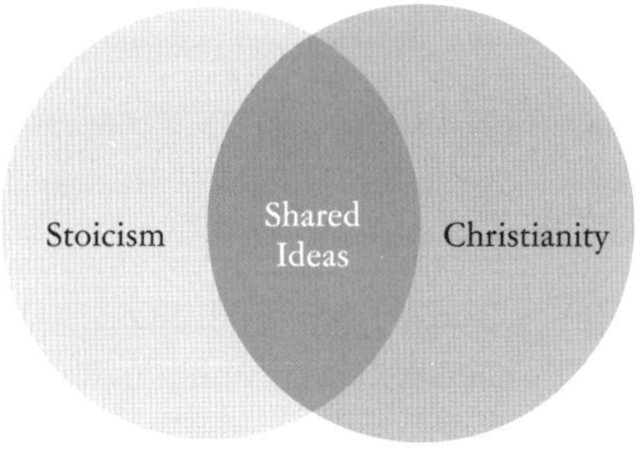

Given these similarities, it's certainly worth our while to examine and appreciate the parallels between these two great traditions. Let's turn our attention briefly to some of these parallels, examining what they are, how they might have occurred, and what they mean for practicing Stoics and Christians today.

A Closer Look at Shared Ideas

Throughout history, many people have been struck by the similarities between Stoicism and Christianity—and this is probably no coincidence. In the century after Jesus's death, his followers were living in a region where Stoicism was the leading philosophy; as one New Testament scholar puts it, "Stoicism had spread throughout the empire before the birth of Jesus and there is little doubt that the soil from which the church sprang up had been watered by the Stoic philosophy."[10] It's a bit like a modern person trying to discuss *government* without referencing *democracy*, or *technology* without talking about *computers*. Even if you avoid mentioning them directly, they are in the back of everyone's minds, and they inform our understanding of the topic whether we like it or not.

In much the same way, Stoicism was in the air in the first-century Mediterranean world. Though there is no suggestion that Jesus himself was influenced by Stoicism, we should remember that his words and works were written down by other people, decades after the crucifixion. As Marcus Borg reminds us:

> Like the historical narratives of the Bible generally, the gospels are the product of a developing tradition, containing earlier and later layers of material and combining history remembered and history

> metaphorized. They preserve the Jesus movement's memory of Jesus and use the language of metaphor and metaphorical narrative to speak about what Jesus had become in their experience, thought, and devotion in the decades after his death.[11]

By suggesting that the followers of Jesus may have been influenced by Stoicism, we are not questioning the originality or authenticity of Jesus, but rather noting the facts on the ground at the time his life was recorded. This understanding is enabling contemporary biblical scholars to freshly interpret the Gospels and Pauline letters. For example, New Testament scholar Runar M. Thorsteinsson observes that "Stoicism could have served as a heuristic key for the audience to properly understand Paul's message—and therefore also . . . Stoicism may serve as a useful tool in our own interpretation of that message."[12] Thus, for Christians, there could be multiple benefits to studying the Bible with Stoicism in mind.

Paul's ethical views seem particularly Stoic-inflected,[13] but scholars also suggest that the authors of Matthew and John may have been influenced by Stoicism in their depictions of Jesus.[14] Theologian and religious historian Stanley K. Stowers proposes that

> The author of the Gospel of Matthew did not identify himself as a Stoic, but that writer understood Stoic ethics and freely adapted elements of Stoic thought in creating his picture of Jesus the moral teacher. This holds especially for the so-called Sermon on the Mount, but it may apply more broadly.[15]

In this view, Matthew was influenced by the Stoic ideal of the sage in crafting his portrayal of Jesus as perfect and holy; he also may have drawn on Stoicism for his ideas about inner perfection and righteousness. Several scholars also find evidence of Stoicism in the Gospel of John, which famously opens with the Greek word *logos*. Eminent classicist (and former priest) Pierre Hadot notes that when Christians of the second century made an effort to present Christianity as a Greco-Roman philosophy—in fact, "as *the* philosophy, the eternal philosophy"—it was possible mainly because of the ambiguity of the word *logos* in John 1.1.[16] The concept of logos was common throughout Greek philosophy, but it was especially associated with Stoicism and serves as a further link between Stoic philosophy and Christianity.

However, it was in the realm of ethics that Stoicism and Christianity overlapped most. Hadot argues that ancient philosophy was primarily a way of life; while beliefs were, of course, important, what mattered most was the way a person interacted with the world. We can see this is true in the surviving writings from the Roman period, in which Stoics constantly encourage themselves or each other to put their ethical principles into practice. Similarly, Jesus continually exhorted his followers to love and care for one another, and Paul's letters to early Christians emphasized the ethical behavior resulting from a true devotion to Christ. These and other ethical similarities have led Thorsteinsson to conclude that

> *Roman Christianity and Roman Stoicism are fundamentally similar in terms of morality or ethics*. This conclusion does not mean that there are no differences whatsoever between the two. Of course there are differences . . . but these are minor variations that do not affect the basic moral agreement seen in the teachings of Roman Christianity and Roman Stoicism.[17]

In general, then, we can say Christianity and Stoicism share a family resemblance, though not a direct genetic inheritance; perhaps we might think of them as cousins stemming from the same family tree. However, even if they were *not* geographically and culturally related, we would still be justified in studying them together for a very basic reason: Many of the great wisdom traditions of the world reach the same conclusions, no matter where and when they come from. They are all distillations of the same human nature, developed *by* and *for* human societies to help people cope with the uncertainties of the world and get along with each other.

Religious scholar (and former nun) Karen Armstrong, in a book comparing the religions that developed between 800 and 200 BC,[18] suggests that as civilizations grew in size and complexity, people needed to find new ways of living together peacefully; the older systems of morality that had worked in small tribes simply didn't work in big cities and complex cultures. Around this time, new forms of spirituality emerged throughout Europe and Asia (notably in Greece, Israel, India, and China) that were devoted to an ethic of compassion:

> The fact that they all came up with such profoundly similar solutions by so many different routes suggests that they had indeed discovered something important about the way human beings worked. Regardless of their theological "beliefs"—which, as we have seen, did not much concern the sages—they all concluded that if people made a disciplined effort to reeducate themselves, they would experience an enhancement of their humanity. In one way or another, their programs were designed to eradicate the egotism that is largely responsible for

our violence, and promoted the empathic spirituality of the Golden Rule.[19]

Clearly, the teachings of Jesus and the Stoics fit into this widespread pattern, representing a highly developed Western expression of compassionate ethics. (Though Jesus was born after 200 BC, Armstrong calls Christianity a "latter-day flowering" of this ethos.[20]) As we will see throughout this book, Stoicism and Christianity both call on their followers to turn the other cheek, to return good for evil, and to love even enemies and strangers.

Small wonder, then, that observers for the past two thousand years have been noting parallels between Stoic and Christian ethics. But it's not all about compassion and non-retaliation. Both traditions also reject greed, hypocrisy, and social display, and both favor inner riches over outer wealth. Here is a quick overview of some basic shared principles:

Both Stoicism and Christianity affirm

- Success defined in internal (spiritual/psychological) terms rather than external (worldly) terms
- Following the example of virtuous role models
- Virtue or righteousness leading to right action in the world

- Consistency between interior attitude and exterior actions
- Internal integrity over outer display or appearance
- Voluntary poverty and sacrifice
- Overcoming temptation and vice through discipline and practice
- Love, fellowship, goodwill
- Compassion toward wrongdoers
- Forgiveness and nonretaliation
- Social harmony and peaceful relations with others
- Spiritual exercises such as prayer and/or meditation
- An uplifted mindset characterized by joy and gratitude
- Letting go of things not in our control
- Seeking deep truth and purpose
- Healing of self and society
- Deep transformation to a new state of being
- Finding and following the right path

Both Stoicism and Christianity reject

- Superficial social conventions
- Arrogance and hypocrisy
- Over-indulgence in pleasures of the flesh
- Selfishness and carelessness toward others
- Physical or emotional violence

As noted by many observers, this way of life is so demanding that it requires an entire revolution in a person's life—as Marcus Borg puts it, "the internal process of dying to an old way of being and entering a new way of being."[21] This conversion is absolutely central to Christianity, but it is also present in a quieter form in Stoicism. Many people don't realize that the conversion experience, which we tend to associate exclusively with religion today, was already present in Greek philosophy. Pierre Hadot suggests that for the ancient Stoics, "philosophy became essentially an act of conversion" requiring "a profound upheaval of the entire being"[22]:

> [Philosophical conversion] corresponds to a complete break with one's habitual way of life: a change in attire and often in diet, sometimes a renunciation of political activities, but above all a total transformation of one's moral life, and the diligent practice of a number of spiritual exercises. In this way the philosopher finds tranquility of the soul, internal freedom—in a word, beatitude.[23]

While Christian conversion is today commonly associated with a *belief* (e.g., accepting Jesus as your savior) or an *emotional experience* (e.g., direct emotional connection with God), the practical result is a complete transformation in a person's *way of being in the world*. As

Marcus Borg reminds us in *Reading the Bible Again for the First Time*:

> Life with God is not about believing certain teachings about God. It is about a covenant—a relationship . . . As the path of life, this relationship is the path of personal transformation. It is the path of liberation from existential, psychological, and spiritual bondage to the lords of convention and culture. It involves dying to an old way of being and being born into a new way of being. It is life lived in accord with radical monotheism: centering one's life in God rather than in the rival lords of culture and convention.[24]

All the great wisdom traditions, in one way or another, insist that the path to blessedness lies in rejecting the false idols of the world (money, power, status) and consciously remaking ourselves in the image of what we believe to be good and holy, whether that is a transcendent or immanent god, or nature, or perhaps simply a complete mystery. Indeed, some people get stuck arguing about the exact nature of the divine—or worse, insisting that their own theological beliefs are right while everyone else's are wrong. But this misses the point that great spiritual leaders have always made: What matters is not *the belief itself* but *the inner transfor-*

mation that results from the belief. If your beliefs provide a profound sense of inner peace, enable you to love your life and other people, and lead you to act in prosocial ways, then you are following in the footsteps of Jesus, Zeno, Epictetus, and the other sages whose wisdom lights our lives.

In their own ways, Jesus and the Stoics lead us to the same place of overcoming our own egos, of shedding our old habits and becoming someone new. And whether or not you agree with every word, I hope you will agree that the parallels between Stoicism and Christianity "suggest there is something here worth taking seriously"—that their similarities "add to the credibility of both."[25] As we read the texts of these two great Western traditions side by side, may you be inspired to live a life of courage, compassion, and devotion to all that is good.

THE PARALLEL TEXTS

TREASURE

What do you value most? Or, to use an expression favored by Jesus and the Stoics, what is your heart set on—external wealth or internal abundance? Material possessions are temporary and will not make you or anyone else happy. Though they appear enticing and hold out the promise of happiness, their promise is false, and their worth is deceptive. This has been proven over and over again throughout history, as many people discover when they accumulate money and are just as miserable as ever.

Instead, the sages tell us, we will be happy when we set our sights (and our hearts) on internal riches: virtue, wisdom, or God. By devoting ourselves to what is truly valuable, we remove the temptations and tribulations of worldly wealth, opening ourselves to inner peace, freedom, and joy. When we choose the path of inner abundance, we give up things of little worth and gain treasure of infinite value.

Which way will you choose? Where will you set your heart?

For where your treasure is, there your heart will be also.

Matthew 6.21

Whatever a person sets their heart on, they naturally love. Now, do people set their hearts on things that are bad? Not at all. And do they take an interest in what does not concern them? No, they do not. It follows, then, that people set their hearts on good things alone, and if they set their hearts on them, they love them too.

EPICTETUS, *DISCOURSES*, 2.22, 1–3

No servant can serve two masters, for either he will hate the one and love the other; or else he will hold to one and despise the other. You aren't able to serve God and money.

LUKE 16.13

If you aim at such great things, you must remember that to attain them requires more than ordinary effort; you will have to give up some things entirely and put off others for the moment. But if you wish for these things also, and at the same time for high positions and wealth, it may be that you will not get even these latter, because you aim also at the former; and certainly you will fail to get the former, which alone bring freedom and happiness.

EPICTETUS, *HANDBOOK*, 1.4

Don't lay up treasures for yourselves on the earth, where moth and rust consume, and where thieves break through and steal; but lay up for yourselves treasures in heaven, where neither moth nor rust consume, and where thieves don't break through and steal.

MATTHEW 6.19–20

Why then are we angry? Because we admire the material things that thieves steal from us. Just cease to admire your clothes, and you will not be angry with the person who steals them.

EPICTETUS, *DISCOURSES*, 1.18, 11

What does it profit a man if he gains the whole world, and loses or forfeits his own self?

Luke 9.25

Great things cannot be bought for small sums; so calculate whether it's preferable to give up your own true self, or merely some of your belongings.

SENECA, *MORAL LETTERS TO LUCILIUS*, 19.4

No one can serve two masters, for either he
will hate the one and love the other, or else he
will be devoted to one and despise the other.
You can't serve both God and money.

MATTHEW 6.24

For where one can say "I" and "mine," to that side each creature must incline; if they are in the flesh, there must the ruling power be; if they are in the moral purpose, there must it be; if they are in externals, there must it be.

EPICTETUS, *DISCOURSES*, 2.22, 19

He said to them, "Beware! Keep yourselves from covetousness, for a man's life doesn't consist of the abundance of the things which he possesses."

LUKE 12.15

One must pay the penalty for all greedy acts, although greed is enough of a penalty in itself. What tears and toil does money wring from us! Greed is wretched in that which it craves and wretched in that which it wins. Think of the daily worry which afflicts every possessor in proportion to the measure of his gain!

SENECA, *MORAL LETTERS TO LUCILIUS*, 115.16

They answered him, "We are Abraham's off-spring, and have never been in bondage to anyone. How do you say, 'You will be made free'?" Jesus answered them, "Most certainly I tell you, everyone who commits sin is the slave of sin."

John 8.33–34

Each man's master is the person who has authority over what he wants or does not want, so as to secure it or take it away. Whoever wants to be free, let him neither wish for anything nor avoid anything that is under the control of others, or else he is necessarily a slave.

Epictetus, *Handbook*, 14.2

VIRTUE/ RIGHTEOUSNESS

When we love what is truly good, we want to align ourselves as closely as possible with that which we love. We discover within ourselves a desire and a capacity to *be* good. The ancient Greeks called this condition virtue, or *aretè* in Greek. Virtue is not primarily about *doing* certain things but about *being* a certain way, cultivating excellence of mind and spirit. For Stoics and later for Christians, performing virtuous actions for others is wonderful, but it's not enough. Our inner intentions must match our outer actions; our internal disposition is what really matters.

Christians educated in the classical tradition incorporated this understanding of virtue into their view of Christ-like ethics—so much so that in the broader culture today, virtue is often synonymous with Christian morality. However, in the Gospels (particularly in Matthew) Jesus prefers to speak of *righteousness* (*dikaiosune*), which implies both right behavior and right relationship with God. Righteousness has theological connotations (with ethics emanating and inseparable from faith), while classical virtue does not.

Despite this difference in theological orientation, virtue and righteousness have marked similarities: they prompt us to overcome our own egos, to consider the needs of others, to think about the big picture rather than immediate gratification. They help us to shine our lights in the world, to produce good fruits, to build our home on a solid foundation—take your pick of metaphors used by Jesus and the Stoics. Whether you focus on righteousness as flowing from faith, or virtue as flowing from reason, may the following passages show you the true abundance of inner goodness.

You are the light of the world. A city located on a hill can't be hidden. Neither do you light a lamp and put it under a measuring basket, but on a stand; and it shines to all who are in the house. Even so, let your light shine before men, that they may see your good works and glorify your Father who is in heaven.

MATTHEW 5.14–16

Doesn't the light of the lamp shine without losing its splendor until it is extinguished? And will the truth and justice and temperance that is in you be extinguished before your death?

MARCUS AURELIUS, *MEDITATIONS*, 12.15

Every good tree produces good fruit, but the corrupt tree produces evil fruit. A good tree can't produce evil fruit, neither can a corrupt tree produce good fruit. Every tree that doesn't grow good fruit is cut down and thrown into the fire. Therefore, by their fruits you will know them.

MATTHEW 7.17–20

Good does not spring from evil, any more than figs grow from olive trees. Things which grow correspond to their seed; and goods cannot depart from their class. Just as that which is honorable does not grow from that which is corrupt, so neither does good grow from evil.

SENECA, *MORAL LETTERS TO LUCILIUS*, 87.25

You are the salt of the earth, but if the salt has lost its flavor, with what will it be salted? It is then good for nothing, but to be cast out and trodden underfoot.

MATTHEW 5.13

Little is needed to ruin and upset everything, only a slight deviation from reason. For the ship's pilot does not need the same amount of preparation to upset his ship that he does to keep it safe; but if he heads a little too much into the wind, he is lost; yes, even if he does nothing wrong intentionally, but merely starts thinking about something else for a moment, he is lost. It is very much the same in life: if you doze even a little, all that you have saved up until now is gone.

EPICTETUS, *DISCOURSES*, 4.3, 4–6

Therefore, you shall be perfect, just as
your Father in heaven is perfect.

MATTHEW 5.48

You know what I mean by a good person?
One who is complete, perfected—whom no
constraint or pressure can render bad.

SENECA, *MORAL LETTERS TO LUCILIUS*, 34.3

Blessed are those who hunger and thirst for righteousness, for they shall be filled.

MATTHEW 5.6

Keep yourself simple, good, pure, serious, free from affectation, a friend of justice, devoted to the gods, kind, affectionate, strenuous in all proper acts. Strive to be such as philosophy wished to make you. Respect the gods and help humankind. Life is short. There is only one fruit of this terrestrial life: a holy disposition and acts that benefit society.

MARCUS AURELIUS, *MEDITATIONS*, 6.30

Now great multitudes were going with him. He turned and said to them, "If anyone comes to me, and doesn't disregard his own father, mother, wife, children, brothers, and sisters, yes, and his own life also, he can't be my disciple."

Luke 14.25–26

That is why the good is preferred above every form of kinship. My father is nothing to me, but only the good. "Are you so hard-hearted?" Yes, that is my nature. This is the coinage which God has given me. For that reason, if the good is something different from the noble and the just, then father and brother and country and all relationships simply disappear. But should I neglect my good, so that you may have it, and should I make way for you? What for? "I am your father." But not a good. "I am your brother." But not a good.

EPICTETUS, *DISCOURSES*, 3.3, 5–7

Blessed are the pure in heart, for they shall see God.

MATTHEW 5.8

Will you, my soul, ever be good and simple and at one and transparent, clearer than the body which surrounds you? Will you never enjoy an affectionate and contented disposition? Will you never be full and without desire of any kind? . . . Will you be satisfied with your present condition, and pleased with all that is around you, and will you convince yourself that you have everything and that it comes from the gods?

Marcus Aurelius, *Meditations*, 10.1

I am the vine. You are the branches. He who remains in me and I in him bears much fruit, for apart from me you can do nothing.

JOHN 15.5

Both humankind and God and the universe produce fruit; at the proper seasons each bears fruit . . . Reason produces fruit both for all and for itself, and also produces other things of the same kind as reason itself.

MARCUS AURELIUS, *MEDITATIONS*, 9.10'

Don't you understand that whatever goes into the
mouth passes into the belly and then out of the body?
But the things which proceed out of the mouth come
out of the heart, and they defile the man. For out of
the heart come evil thoughts, murders, adulteries,
sexual sins, thefts, false testimony, and blasphemies.
These are the things which defile the man; but to
eat with unwashed hands doesn't defile the man.

MATTHEW 15.17–20

The primary and highest purity is that which appears in the mind, and the same is true of impurity. But you would not find the same impurity in a mind as you would in a body, and since it is mind, what else would you find impure about it than that which makes it dirty for the performance of its own functions? And the functions of a mind are the exercise of choice, of refusal, of desire, of aversion, of preparation, of purpose, and of assent. What makes the mind dirty and unclean in these functions? Nothing but its bad decisions. It follows, therefore, that impurity of a mind consists of bad judgments, and purification consists in creating within it the proper kind of judgments. A pure mind is one that has the proper kind of judgments.

EPICTETUS, *DISCOURSES*, 4.11, 5–8

Out of the abundance of the heart, the mouth speaks. The good man out of his good treasure brings out good things, and the evil man out of his evil treasure brings out evil things. I tell you that every idle word that men speak, they will give account of it in the day of judgment. For by your words you will be justified, and by your words you will be condemned.

MATTHEW 12.34–37

Conform to justice, that you may always speak the truth freely and without disguise. Do what agrees with the law and accords with the worth of each thing. And do not be obstructed by anyone else's errors or words or deeds.

MARCUS AURELIUS, *MEDITATIONS*, 12.1

If your right eye causes you to stumble, pluck it out and throw it away from you. For it is more profitable for you that one of your members should perish than for your whole body to be cast into hell. If your right hand causes you to stumble, cut it off, and throw it away from you. For it is more profitable for you that one of your members should perish, than for your whole body to be cast into hell.

MATTHEW 5.29–30

Short is the time which remains of your life. Live as if you were on a mountain. For it makes no difference whether you live there or here, if you regard everywhere in the world as the community of humankind. Let people see, let them know a real man who lives according to nature. If they cannot endure him, let them kill him. For it is better to die than to live as they do.

MARCUS AURELIUS, *MEDITATIONS*, 10.15

For everyone who does evil hates the light and doesn't come to the light, lest his works would be exposed. But he who does the truth comes to the light, that his works may be revealed, that they have been done in God.

JOHN 3.20–21

When you close your doors and make darkness within, remember never to say you are alone, for you are not alone; God is within, and your own guardian spirit. And what need do they have of light to see what you're doing?

EPICTETUS, *DISCOURSES*, 1.14, 13–14

Blessed are your eyes, for they see; and your ears, for they hear. For most certainly I tell you that many prophets and righteous men desired to see the things which you see, and didn't see them; and to hear the things which you hear, and didn't hear them.

MATTHEW 13.16-17

Do not be ungrateful for these gifts, and do not be forgetful of better things. Give thanks to God for sight and hearing and, by Zeus, for life itself and for what is conducive to it, for dry fruits, for wine, for olive oil. At the same time, remember that he has given you something better than all these things—the faculty which can make use of them, pass judgment upon them, estimate the value of each.

EPICTETUS, *DISCOURSES*, 2.23, 5–6

The lamp of the body is the eye. When your eye is good, your whole body is also full of light; but when it is evil, your body also is full of darkness. Therefore, see whether the light that is in you isn't darkness. If, therefore, your whole body is full of light, having no part dark, it will be wholly full of light, as when the lamp with its bright shining gives you light.

LUKE 11.34–36

There is no one, I tell you, who would not burn with love for this vision of virtue, if only they had the privilege of seeing it. At present, there are many things that cut off our vision, piercing it with too strong a light, or clogging it with too much darkness. But if, just as certain drugs are used for sharpening and clearing the eyesight, we are willing to free our mind's eye from hindrances, we will be able to perceive virtue even if it is buried—even if poverty stands in the way, and even if lowliness and disgrace block the path. We will then behold that true beauty.

SENECA, *MORAL LETTERS TO LUCILIUS*, 115.6

SOCIAL HARMONY

Humans are social creatures. This simple fact of life has profound implications for ethics: We may sometimes feel that we can't live with other people, but we certainly can't live *without* them. The key to a happy life is figuring out how to get along with others in a way that is fair and respectful.

Both Stoic and Christian ethics are well-known for their doctrine of personal sacrifice in favor of other people. Jesus is constantly—constantly!—admonishing his listeners to give up their own material wealth and egotistical concerns, donating to the poor and humbling themselves in social settings. Likewise, the Stoics say we should promote the common good even at the cost of our own social position, material comfort, or even, in certain circumstances, our own life.

Interestingly, both Jesus and the Stoics insist that they are not making radical new demands on society and individuals, but that they are returning to ancient, established principles—Jesus to the law of Israel, and the Stoics to the law of nature. They typically claimed that their contemporaries had strayed far from authentic morality, and they were merely trying to guide people back to the true path. For these sages, what mattered was not the letter of the law but its spirit. When we act, do we do so with integrity and generosity? When we gather with others, do we place their needs equal to or above our own? Do we treat other people the way we want to be treated?

We might sometimes feel that it's pointless for us to practice these principles when so many people around us clearly do not. However, for both Christians and Stoics, what matters is that we stick to our beliefs, regardless of what others do. Even when it's hard, even when everyone around us is doing otherwise, we can stay true to our values by trying to act like our role models (such as Jesus or Epictetus) would act. And fortunately for us, they left us their wise words for guidance. May these words help you find social harmony in your own life—no matter how difficult it is.

Don't think that I came to destroy the law or the prophets. I didn't come to destroy, but to fulfill.

MATTHEW 5.17

"Yes, but these arguments make men despise the laws." No, these arguments make those who adopt them obedient to the laws. Law is not just what any fool can do. See how these arguments make us behave rightly even towards our critics, since they teach us to claim nothing against these people in which they can surpass us.

EPICTETUS, *DISCOURSES*, 4.7, 33–34

Then the righteous will answer him, saying, "Lord, when did we see you hungry and feed you, or thirsty and give you a drink? When did we see you as a stranger and take you in, or naked and clothe you? When did we see you sick or in prison and come to you?"

The King will answer them, "Most certainly I tell you, because you did it to one of the least of these my brothers, you did it to me."

Matthew 25.37–40

Nature produced us as kin to one another, since she created us from the same source and to the same end. She created in us mutual affection and made us prone to friendships. She established fairness and justice; according to her ruling, it is worse to commit an injury than to suffer injury. Through her orders, let our hands be ready for all who need to be helped.

SENECA, *MORAL LETTERS TO LUCILIUS*, 95.52

Again you have heard that it was said to the ancient ones, "You shall not make false vows, but shall perform to the Lord your vows," but I tell you, don't swear at all: neither by heaven, for it is the throne of God; nor by the earth, for it is the footstool of his feet; nor by Jerusalem, for it is the city of the great King. Neither shall you swear by your head, for you can't make one hair white or black. But let your "Yes" be "Yes" and your "No" be "No." Whatever is more than these is of the evil one.

MATTHEW 5.33–37

Undertake your duties with willingness, with an eye to the common interest, with due consideration, and without distraction; do not dress up your thoughts in flowery language, and do not use too many words, or be busy with too many things . . . Be cheerful, and do not seek external help or depend on other people for your tranquility. A person should stand upright, not be kept upright by others.

MARCUS AURELIUS, *MEDITATIONS*, 3.5

Blessed are the peacemakers, for they
will be called children of God.

Matthew 5.9

A wise and good person neither quarrels with anyone nor, as far as possible, allows others to quarrel.

EPICTETUS, *DISCOURSES*, 4.5, 1

When you are invited to a feast, go and sit in the lowest place, so that when he who invited you comes, he may tell you, "Friend, move up higher." Then you will be honored in the presence of all who sit at the table with you. For everyone who exalts himself will be humbled, and whoever humbles himself will be exalted.

LUKE 14.10–11

Has someone been honored above you at a dinner party, or in salutation, or in being called on to give advice? Now, if these things are good, you should be happy this person got them; but if they are not good, don't be distressed because you didn't get them. Bear in mind that, if you don't act the same way that others do, with a view to getting things that are not under your control, you cannot expect to receive an equal share of them.

EPICTETUS, *HANDBOOK*, 25.1

Whatever you desire for men to do to you, you shall also do to them; for this is the law and the prophets.

MATTHEW 7.12

As you yourself are part of a social system, so let every act of yours be a part of social life. Whenever you act with no reference, either directly or indirectly, to a social end, you tear your life apart and prevent it from being whole.

MARCUS AURELIUS, *MEDITATIONS*, 9.23

SINCERITY

Arrogance and hypocrisy are ancient problems. Because humans naturally care for other people, many of us also care what other people think about us. This tendency can be healthy when it helps keep selfish desires in check—for example, you don't make a scene because you care what other people think about you—but it becomes a problem when you crave the admiration of others. In ancient times, just as today, some people tried to elevate themselves in society by any means possible, whether through wealth, social status, or trying to seem holier than thou.

Jesus was extremely critical of hypocritical people, and his greatest ire was directed toward certain Jewish leaders of his time, the Pharisees. According to Jesus and the Gospel writers (particularly Matthew), these men were fanatically concerned with external appearances, including ritual cleanliness, but ignored the true human need all around them. Jesus's interactions with them proved over and over again that what mattered wasn't the performance of rituals but healing people, caring for the poor, and bringing political and religious peace to communities.

Likewise, the ancient Stoics consistently called on people to forget about external appearances and focus on what genuinely matters: cultivating their own character through rational and sociable action. Epictetus, in particular, ridiculed the men he thought were vain, insincere, and too concerned with other people's opinions. Roman society, like our own, was extremely materialistic and focused on career success, social status, and wealth creation. The Stoics were very consistent in their message to downplay these corrupting temptations and focus on living authentically, staying true to one's principles, and practicing humility rather than arrogance.

These calls to *genuine* rather than *superficial* or *insincere* concern for other people have echoed down the centuries. Very few of us will reach Jesus's level of care for the poor or achieve Zeno's austere lifestyle, but we can make sincere efforts to match our actions to our words. These ethical luminaries remind us to engage honestly and meaningfully with others—being forthright, direct, and showing what is truly in our hearts.

There is nothing covered up that will not be revealed, nor hidden that will not be known. Therefore, whatever you have said in the darkness will be heard in the light. What you have spoken in the ear in the inner rooms will be proclaimed on the housetops.

LUKE 12.2–3

What profit is there in hiding ourselves away and avoiding the eyes and ears of other people? A good conscience welcomes the crowd, but a bad conscience is disturbed and troubled even in solitude. If your deeds are honorable, let everybody know them; if bad, what does it matter that no one else knows them, since you yourself know them?

SENECA, *MORAL LETTERS TO LUCILIUS*, 43.4–5

When you fast, don't be like the hypocrites, with sad faces. For they disfigure their faces that they may be seen by men to be fasting. Most certainly, I tell you, they have received their reward. But you, when you fast, anoint your head and wash your face, so that you are not seen by men to be fasting, but by your Father, who is in secret; and your Father, who sees in secret, will reward you.

MATTHEW 6.16–18

For this reason, Euphrates was right in saying, "For a long time I tried not to be known as a philosopher, and this was useful to me. For I knew that what I did rightly was done for my own sake and not for the spectators: it was for myself that I ate rightly and was modest in my aspect and my gait: all was for myself and God . . . For this reason, those who did not know my design wondered how it was that, though I was familiar and conversant with all philosophers, I was not a philosopher myself. What harm is there in the philosopher being discovered by my acts, and not by outward signs?"

EPICTETUS, *DISCOURSES*, 4.8, 17–20

When you pray, you shall not be as the hypocrites, for they love to stand and pray in the synagogues and in the corners of the streets, that they may be seen by men. Most certainly, I tell you, they have received their reward. But you, when you pray, enter into your inner room, and having shut your door, pray to your Father, who is in secret; and your Father, who sees in secret, will reward you openly.

Matthew, 6.5-6

How foolish people are! They whisper the most dishonorable prayers to heaven, but if anyone listens, they are silent at once. They communicate to God that which they are unwilling for other people to know. Don't you think some wholesome advice like this could be given to you: "Live with other people as if God were watching; speak with God as if other people were listening"?

SENECA, *MORAL LETTERS TO LUCILIUS*, 10.5

He who is faithful in a very little is faithful also in much. He who is dishonest in a very little is also dishonest in much. If, therefore, you have not been faithful in unrighteous property, who will commit to your trust the true riches?

LUKE 16.10–11

Do you wish me to make a deposit with you, when you have dishonored your own moral purpose and aimed to get a bit of cash, or some high position, or advancement at court? . . . Show yourself to me as a faithful, respectful, dependable person; show that your judgments are those of a friend, and you'll see how I won't wait for you to entrust knowledge of your affairs to me—I'll go of my own accord and ask you to hear about mine. For who despises a friendly and faithful counsellor?

EPICTETUS, *DISCOURSES*, 4.13, 14–16

He also spoke this parable to certain people who were convinced of their own righteousness, and who despised all others: "Two men went up into the temple to pray; one was a Pharisee, and the other was a tax collector. The Pharisee stood and prayed by himself like this: 'God, I thank you that I am not like the rest of men: extortionists, unrighteous, adulterers, or even like this tax collector. I fast twice a week. I give tithes of all that I get.' But the tax collector, standing far away, wouldn't even lift up his eyes to heaven, but beat his chest, saying, 'God, be merciful to me, a sinner!' I tell you, this man went down to his house justified rather than the other; for everyone who exalts himself will be humbled, but he who humbles himself will be exalted."

LUKE 18.9–14

When such are the people we live among—so confused, so ignorant of what they are saying, unaware of what vice they possess, or how they came to have it, or how they will get rid of it—among such people I wonder whether it isn't worthwhile for us to examine ourselves, asking these questions: "Is it possible that I too am one of these people? What impression do I have of myself? How do I conduct myself? Do I act like a wise person? Do I act with self-control? Am I conscious, as the person who knows nothing should be, that I know nothing?"

EPICTETUS, *DISCOURSES*, 2.21, 8–10

Then Jesus spoke to the multitudes and to his disciples, saying, "The scribes and the Pharisees sit on Moses's seat. All things therefore they tell you to observe, observe and do, but don't do their works; for they say, and don't do. For they bind heavy burdens that are grievous to be borne and lay them on men's shoulders; but they themselves will not lift a finger to help them. But they do all their works to be seen by men . . . They love the place of honor at feasts, the best seats in the synagogues, the salutations in the marketplaces, and to be called 'Rabbi, Rabbi' by men."

Matthew 23.1–7

Whenever you see another person holding office, set against this the fact that you possess the ability to get along without office; whenever you see someone with wealth, look at what you have instead. For if you have nothing instead, you are certainly miserable; but if you have this—that you have no need of wealth—know that you are better off and have something much more valuable.

EPICTETUS, *DISCOURSES*, 4.9, 1–2

In the hearing of all the people, he said to his disciples,
"Beware of those scribes who like to walk in long robes,
and love greetings in the marketplaces, the best seats
in the synagogues, and the best places at feasts; who
devour widows' houses, and for a pretense make long
prayers. These will receive greater condemnation."

LUKE 20.45–47

No man has treated humankind worse than he who has studied philosophy as if it were some marketable trade, and who lives in a different manner from that which he advises. For those who commit every fault which they condemn in others, advertise themselves as patterns of useless training.

SENECA, *MORAL LETTERS TO LUCILIUS*, 108.36

The Lord said to him, "Now you Pharisees cleanse the outside of the cup and of the platter, but your inward part is full of extortion and wickedness. You foolish ones, didn't he who made the outside make the inside also?"

LUKE 11.39–40

Let us say what we feel and feel what we say; let speech harmonize with life. The good person should be the same when you see them and when you hear them.

SENECA, *MORAL LETTERS TO LUCILIUS*, 75.4

In praying, don't use vain repetitions as the Gentiles do; for they think that they will be heard for their much speaking. Therefore, don't be like them, for your Father knows what things you need before you ask him.

MATTHEW 6.7–8

A prayer of the Athenians: Rain, rain, O dear Zeus, down on the ploughed fields of the Athenians and on the plains. In truth, we ought not to pray at all, or we ought to pray in this simple and noble way.

MARCUS AURELIUS, *MEDITATIONS*, 5.7

Don't judge according to appearance,
but judge righteous judgment.

JOHN 7.24

Don't you know that a good and excellent person does nothing for the sake of appearances, but only for the sake of having acted right?

EPICTETUS, *DISCOURSES*, 3.24, 50

COMPASSION & MERCY

Compassion and mercy are not the first words that come to mind when many people think of Stoicism, but perhaps they should be. The Stoics, like Jesus, are forcefully concerned with being merciful to those who err and gracious even to those who hate them. In fact, this is the area where scholars find the most direct connection between Stoicism and Christianity. Speaking of the Sermon on the Mount (Matthew 5–7), in which Jesus commands his disciples to love their enemies, theologian and scholar Stanley K. Stowers notes:

> The command to imitate God in this respect is central to the thought of the sermon as a whole. God's love is for all. Much has been made of Lev 19:18 in Matt 5:43, but no Jewish text interprets it as commanding the love of enemies, and scholars usually admit that the idea is not present there in [the Old Testament book] Leviticus. When one looks

> for both the idea of love or benevolence toward enemies and the kind of reasoning that supports the idea here, the evidence for this odd idea strongly points to Stoicism..[26]

The Stoics were famous in antiquity for their principles of universal love and non-retaliation. Following Socrates—who didn't hold grudges against his fellow citizens even when they wrongfully imprisoned (and later executed) him—the Stoics believed people do wrong through ignorance; these unfortunate souls mistakenly think that egotistical actions will benefit them, when the opposite is true. Such a terrible error calls for compassion and guidance, not anger and revenge.

Jesus, too, regularly taught mercy and compassion. Consistent with his stance against hypocrisy, he reminded people that no one is sinless and therefore no one is in a position to judge others; only God can do that. Paired with his radical message of love, forgiveness, and reconciliation, Jesus created a supremely charitable ethic that has inspired and challenged his followers ever since.

As you read the compassionate words of Jesus and the Stoics, I encourage you to reflect on ways you can bring more benevolence and understanding into your own life. We all have space to become more charitable, to judge less and sympathize more. What will you do today to bring more compassion into your life?

Don't judge, so that you won't be judged. For with whatever judgment you judge, you will be judged; and with whatever measure you measure, it will be measured to you.

MATTHEW 7.1–2

Consider that you also do many things wrong, and that you are a person like everyone else; and even if you abstain from certain faults, you still have the disposition to commit them.

MARCUS AURELIUS, *MEDITATIONS*, 11.18

You have heard that it was said to the ancient ones, "You shall not murder," and "Whoever murders will be in danger of the judgment." But I tell you that everyone who is angry with his brother without a cause will be in danger of the judgment. Whoever says to his brother, "Raca!" will be in danger of the council. Whoever says, "You fool!" will be in danger of the fire of hell.

MATTHEW 5.21–22

Why are you angry with her, because the poor woman has gone astray in the greatest matters, and has been transformed from a human being into a viper? Why don't you, if anything, pity her instead? As we pity the blind and the lame, why do we not pity those who have been made blind and lame in their governing faculties? . . . Whoever remembers this will not be enraged at anyone, will not be angry with anyone, will not criticize anyone, will not blame, nor hate, nor offend anyone.

EPICTETUS, *DISCOURSES*, 1.28, 9–10

Be merciful, even as your Father is also merciful.

LUKE 6.36

To scheme how to bite back someone who bites and to return evil for evil is the act not of a human being but of a wild beast . . . But to be a source of good hope to those who wrong us is characteristic of a benevolent and civilized way of life.

MUSONIUS RUFUS, *LECTURES*, 10.5

You have heard that it was said, "You shall love your neighbor and hate your enemy." But I tell you, love your enemies, bless those who curse you, do good to those who hate you, and pray for those who mistreat you and persecute you, that you may be children of your Father who is in heaven. For he makes his sun to rise on the evil and the good, and sends rain on the just and the unjust.

MATTHEW 5.43–45

If you can, correct those who do wrong; but if you cannot, remember that compassion is given to you for this purpose. The gods, too, are compassionate to such people, for sometimes they even help them obtain health, wealth, reputation. And it's in your power to do the same; or tell me, who is stopping you?

MARCUS AURELIUS, *MEDITATIONS*, 9.11

The scribes and the Pharisees brought a woman taken in adultery. Having set her in the middle, they told him, "Teacher, we found this woman in adultery, in the very act. Now, in our law, Moses commanded us to stone such women. What then do you say about her?" They said this testing him, that they might have something to accuse him of.

But Jesus stooped down and wrote on the ground with his finger. When they continued asking him, he looked up and said to them, "He who is without sin among you, let him throw the first stone at her."

John 8.3–7

"What!" you say. "Shouldn't this robber and this adulterer to be put to death?" Not at all, but you should ask rather, "Should this man to be put to death who is in a state of error and delusion about the greatest matters, and is in a state of blindness—not in the vision which distinguishes between white and black, but in the judgment which distinguishes between good and evil?" And if you put it this way, you will realize how inhuman a sentiment it is that you are uttering . . . Drop this readiness to take offence and this spirit of hatred.

EPICTETUS, *DISCOURSES*, 1.18, 5–9

Blessed are the merciful, for they shall obtain mercy.

MATTHEW 5.7

It is a special gift of humans to love
even those who do wrong.

MARCUS AURELIUS, *MEDITATIONS*, 7.22

Why do you see the speck of chaff that is in your brother's eye, but don't consider the beam that is in your own eye? Or how can you tell your brother, "Brother, let me remove the speck of chaff that is in your eye," when you yourself don't see the beam that is in your own eye? You hypocrite! First, remove the beam from your own eye, and then you can see clearly to remove the speck of chaff that is in your brother's eye.

LUKE 6.41–42

If we desire to be impartial judges of all that takes place, we must first convince ourselves that no one is faultless, because this is what causes most of our indignation. "I have not sinned; I have done no wrong." Say, rather, you do not *admit* that you have done any wrong. We are infuriated at being corrected, either by reprimand or actual punishment, even though we are sinning at that very time, and adding insolence and obstinacy to our wrongdoing. Who can honestly declare that they have broken no laws?

SENECA, *ON ANGER*, 2.28

Blessed are those who have been persecuted for righteousness' sake, for theirs is the Kingdom of Heaven.

MATTHEW 5.10

Suppose that men kill you, cut you in pieces, curse you. What then can these things do to prevent your mind from remaining pure, wise, steady, just?

MARCUS AURELIUS, *MEDITATIONS*, 8.51

"A man was going down from Jerusalem to Jericho, when he was attacked by robbers. They stripped him of his clothes, beat him, and went away, leaving him half dead. A priest happened to be going down the same road, and when he saw the man, he passed by on the other side. So too, a Levite, when he came to the place and saw him, passed by on the other side. But a certain Samaritan, as he traveled, came where the man was. When he saw him, he was moved with compassion, came to him, and bound up his wounds, pouring on oil and wine. He set him on his own animal, brought him to an inn, and took care of him. On the next day, when he departed, he took out two denarii, gave them to the host, and said to him, 'Take care of him. Whatever you spend beyond that, I will repay you when I return.' Now, which of these three do you think seemed to be a neighbor to him who fell among the robbers?" He said, "He who showed mercy on him." Then Jesus said to him, "Go and do likewise."

LUKE 10.30–37

Our Stoic philosophers say we must be in motion up to the very end of our life; we will never cease to labor for the general good, to help individual people, and to provide assistance even to our enemies.

SENECA, *ON LEISURE*, 1.4

Why do you see the speck that is in your brother's eye,
but don't consider the beam that is in your own eye?
Or how will you tell your brother, 'Let me remove
the speck from your eye,' and behold, the beam is in
your own eye? You hypocrite! First, remove the beam
out of your own eye, and then you can see clearly
to remove the speck out of your brother's eye.

MATTHEW 7.3–5

Do not preach right-doing to people who are aware of your wrongdoing.

MUSONIUS RUFUS, *SAYINGS*, 32

Don't judge, and you won't be judged.
Don't condemn, and you won't be condemned. Set free, and you will be set free.

Luke 6.37

When you are offended at any person's fault, immediately look at yourself and reflect how you yourself err in a similar manner; for example, in thinking that money is a good thing, or pleasure, or a bit of reputation, and the like. By thinking about this, you will quickly forget your anger.

MARCUS AURELIUS, *MEDITATIONS*, 10.30

FORGIVENESS & RECONCILIATION

It's one of the hardest ethical imperatives of all: forgiving those who wrong you and even being reconciled to them despite these wrongs. But the great sages have always insisted this is necessary—not just to benefit the other person, but for your own sake as well. We are happier and more at peace when we release all that potential anger and do not allow it to fester within our spirit. By forgiving those who wrong us, we help heal ourselves, the other person (or group of people), and even our society as a whole.

Interestingly, the Stoics did not officially advocate forgiveness, as they suggested no one else has the power to truly injure us. (In Stoic doctrine, good and bad lie within our own character, which is not vulnerable to other people's actions. Of course, others may harm our body and worldly possessions, but our happiness does not depend on these things.) This idea is well illustrated in the following passage from Seneca's *On the Constancy of the Wise Person*:

> But what will the wise person do when they are hit? They will do as Cato did when he was struck in the face; he did not flare up and revenge the outrage; he did not even pardon it, but ignored it, showing more magnanimity in not acknowledging it than if he had forgiven it. (14.3)

Technically speaking, for a Stoic sage, there is never a reason to forgive because true harm can never be perpetrated against them. However, since most of us are still far away from perfect wisdom, we may still feel the sting of insults and injuries (though hopefully not as much as we used to). Therefore, we still need to forgive others and make our peace with them.

For Christians, Jesus is the ultimate avatar of God's forgiveness: not only did he sacrifice his earthly life to atone for the sins of humanity, but even on the cross, he asked God to forgive those who crucified him. Jesus also commanded his disciples to forgive other people, whether the transgressor be a stranger or a brother. Sometimes it's hardest to forgive those who are closest to us: we feel a greater sense of betrayal, that they should have cared more about us, that they should have known how their actions would make us feel. But Jesus insisted that we forgive them anyway. He also placed personal forgiveness above the performance of religious rituals, making it clear that the path to spiritual perfection lies not in ceremony but in clemency.

As we ponder these ideas today, we might wonder whether it is better to stay angry in order to fight for justice for ourselves or others. This argument—that righteous anger is necessary for rectitude—goes back at least to Aristotle and probably to the beginning of humankind. However, both Jesus and the Stoics declare that forgiveness and reconciliation is the better path. Justice, while desirable, will always remain beyond our grasp in this world; though it's worth working for, it's not worth sacrificing our souls for. Those who stay angry end up wasting away from the inside, making bad decisions and giving into the desire for revenge.

Forgiveness, on the other hand, is well within our capabilities and has the guaranteed consequence of making us happier—and in the long run, it will likely contribute to justice and social harmony. So why not go for it? If you're on the fence about forgiveness, try it and see how things work out for you. (Should it make your life worse, you can always go back to being angry again!) Read on for more encouragement in the gentle art of forgiveness.

If you forgive men their trespasses, your heavenly Father will also forgive you. But if you don't forgive men their trespasses, neither will your Father forgive your trespasses.

MATTHEW 6.14–15

When someone does you wrong, immediately consider with what opinion about good or evil they have done wrong. When you see this, you will pity that person and be neither surprised nor angry. For you yourself think the same thing to be good that they do, or else another thing of the same kind. It is your duty then to pardon this person.

Marcus Aurelius, *Meditations*, 7.26

One of the multitude said to him, "Teacher, tell my brother to divide the inheritance with me." But he said to him, "Man, who made me a judge or an arbitrator over you?"

LUKE 12.13–14

"My brother should not have treated me so." No, but it's for him to look to that. As for me, no matter how he behaves, I will deal with him as I should. For this is my own business: that belongs to another.

EPICTETUS, *DISCOURSES*, 3.10, 19

You have heard that it was said, “An eye for an eye, and a tooth for a tooth.” But I tell you, don’t resist him who is evil; but whoever strikes you on your right cheek, turn to him the other also.

MATTHEW 5.38–39

It is not honorable to repay injuries with injuries, though it is honorable to repay benefits with benefits . . . Revenge and retaliation are words people use and even think to be righteous, yet they do not greatly differ from wrongdoing, except in the order in which they are done: he who renders pain for pain has more excuse for his sin; that is all.

Seneca, *On Anger*, 2.32

Then Peter came and said to him, "Lord, how often shall my brother sin against me, and I forgive him? Until seven times?" Jesus said to him, "I don't tell you until seven times, but until seventy times seven."

MATTHEW 18.21–22

Will you not bear with your own brother, who has Zeus for his forefather, and is born of the same seed as you and is of the same heavenly descent?

EPICTETUS, *DISCOURSES*, 1.13, 3

If, therefore, you are offering your gift at the altar, and there remember that your brother has anything against you, leave your gift there before the altar, and go your way. First be reconciled to your brother, and then come and offer your gift.

Matthew 5.23–24

If we define the good as consisting in right moral purpose, then the mere preservation of our relationships becomes a good; and furthermore, the person who gives up some of their external things achieves the good. "My father is taking away my money." But he is doing you no harm. "My brother is going to get the larger part of the farm." Let him have all he wants. That doesn't help him at all to get a part of your decency, does it, or of your fidelity, or of your brotherly love?

EPICTETUS, *DISCOURSES*, 3.3, 8–9

But I tell you who hear: love your enemies, do good to those who hate you, bless those who curse you, and pray for those who mistreat you. To him who strikes you on the cheek, offer also the other; and from him who takes away your cloak, don't withhold your coat also.

Luke 6.27–29

Where is there any room for contention, then, if a man is in such a state of mind? Is he amazed at anything that happens? Does anything take him by surprise? Does he not expect worse and harsher treatment from the wicked than actually befalls him? Does he not count it as gain whenever they fail to go to the limit? "So-and-so criticized you." I'm greatly obliged to him for not striking me. "Yes, but he struck you, too." I'm greatly obliged to him for not wounding me. "Yes, but he wounded you, too." I'm greatly obliged to him for not killing me. For when, or from what teacher, did he learn that man is a gentle and sociable creature and that wrongdoing in itself does great harm to the wrongdoer?

EPICTETUS, *DISCOURSES*, 4.5, 8–10

GENEROSITY

Generosity has many aspects: we can give time, money, emotional support, professional expertise, or anything else we have. But what matters in every case is the manner and attitude of our giving, not the amount. It's much better to give unpretentiously and straight from the heart than to give with much fanfare, expecting recognition or even reward.

In ancient times, as in our own, many people made donations just to be recognized as generous by others, which, of course, is not true generosity. Jesus tells his followers to be so discreet in their giving that the left hand does not even know what the right hand is doing. Marcus Aurelius says that generosity is simply the flowering of the proper human spirit, and nothing to get puffed up with pride about. Just as we should not make public displays of virtue or righteousness, we should not be generous for the sake of appearances.

But Jesus and the Stoics go even further than this. They say we should not give in order to feel good about ourselves—even thinking to yourself how generous you are negates your generosity! We should give to others simply because we care about them and want the best for them. True generosity is the overflow of an abundant spirit. If we have properly cultivated love for others, benefits will flow naturally from us.

For some of us, however, the direction goes the other way: generosity is a stepping stone on the path toward love. We often learn to love others by taking care of them. When we show generosity to others, this means they are in our thoughts, and we are making efforts to benefit them. Therefore, Jesus and the Stoics encourage us to be charitable even when we don't feel like it. Our acts of goodwill can help us cultivate an open and loving spirit.

Jesus sat down opposite the treasury and saw how the multitude cast money into the treasury. Many who were rich cast in much. A poor widow came and she cast in two small brass coins, which equal a quadrans coin. He called his disciples to himself and said to them, "Most certainly I tell you, this poor widow gave more than all those who are giving into the treasury, for they all gave out of their abundance, but she, out of her poverty, gave all that she had to live on."

MARK 12.41–44

We prize much more what comes from a willing hand than what comes from a full one. This man has given me but little, yet he could not afford more. That one has given much, but he hesitated, he put it off, he grumbled when he gave it, he gave it haughtily, or he proclaimed it aloud, and did it to please others, not to please the person to whom he gave it . . . We must not consider how great presents are, but in what spirit they are given.

SENECA, *ON BENEFITS*, 1.7–9

If anyone sues you to take away your coat, let him have your cloak also. Whoever compels you to go one mile, go with him two. Give to him who asks you, and don't turn away him who desires to borrow from you.

MATTHEW 5.40–42

However quick he may be, a man gives too late when he must be asked to give. We should, instead, guess what each person needs, and when we have discovered this, set them free from the hard necessity of asking. You may be sure that a benefit which comes unasked will be delightful and will not be forgotten.

SENECA, *ON BENEFITS*, 2.2

Be careful that you don't do your charitable giving before men, to be seen by them, or else you have no reward from your Father who is in heaven. Therefore, when you do merciful deeds, don't sound a trumpet before yourself, as the hypocrites do in the synagogues and in the streets, that they may get glory from men. Most certainly, I tell you, they have received their reward. But when you do merciful deeds, don't let your left hand know what your right hand does, so that your merciful deeds may be in secret, then your Father who sees in secret will reward you openly.

Matthew 6.1–4

When you have done a good act and another has received it, why do you look for a third thing besides these, as fools do, either to have the reputation of having done a good act or to obtain something in return?

MARCUS AURELIUS, *MEDITATIONS*, 7.73

Give to everyone who asks you, and don't ask him who takes away your goods to give them back again. As you would like people to do to you, do exactly so to them.

Luke 6.30–31

Let us give in the way in which we ourselves should like to receive. Above all, we should give willingly, quickly, and without any hesitation.

SENECA, *On Benefits*, 2.1

Give, and it will be given to you: good measure, pressed down, shaken together, and running over, will be given to you. For with the same measure you measure, it will be measured back to you.

LUKE 6.38

I will view all lands as though they belong to me, and my own as though they belonged to all humankind. I will live so as to remember that I was born for others, and will thank Nature on this account: for how could she have done better for me? She has given me alone to all, and all to me alone. Whatever I may possess, I will neither hoard it greedily nor squander it recklessly. I will think that I have no possessions so real as those I have given away to deserving people.

SENECA, *ON THE HAPPY LIFE*, 20.3–4

LOVE

Christianity is well known for teaching love—didn't Jesus say the two greatest commandments are to love God and to love other people? But it's less well known how much Stoicism emphasizes love. In fact, love is intrinsic to Stoic theory, baked deep into core philosophical principles such as *oikeiosis* (appropriation) and living in accordance with nature.[27] All the writings we have from the Roman Stoics express how important love is for human flourishing. Love is a normal, necessary, and expected part of our lives.

However, both Jesus and the Stoics knew there are competing interests in the human heart that sometimes pull us in the opposite direction, toward strife, contempt, hatred, and opposition. That's why they urge us so insistently to love—and not just our friends and family, but even people outside our tribe, even strangers, even would-be enemies. Jesus astonished the Pharisees by eating with tax collectors and sinners, just as Marcus Aurelius astonished the Roman senators by not executing or punishing those who rebelled against him. The command to love is a serious one—sometimes even a matter of life or death.

So how do we learn to love like Jesus and Marcus? It may help to remind ourselves that love is not a feeling that comes and goes, but rather a consistent and effortful attitude toward other people. Popular culture often suggests that love is a strong emotion that just *happens* to us. But the great wisdom traditions say otherwise. Loving others takes a lot of work. It's difficult and very tiresome to redirect our impulses away from selfish ends and toward love. We have to lay the groundwork through continuous study and practice. If we find ourselves coming up short on love, it doesn't mean we're naturally deficient; it just means we need more preparation.

I encourage you to see the wise words that follow as an invitation to *practice* love. Perhaps you can think of a single person or situation that calls for your practice. Perhaps you want to meditate on universal love or pray for the well-being of those who seek to harm you. However you choose to practice love, remember you can always come back to Jesus and the Stoics for guidance and encouragement.

I command these things to you, that
you may love one another.

JOHN 15.17

Love humankind.

MARCUS AURELIUS, *MEDITATIONS*, 7.31

A new commandment I give to you, that you love one another. Just as I have loved you, you also love one another.

John 13.34

Adapt yourself to the things that circumstances have brought to you. And the people who happen to surround you—love them, but do it truly, sincerely.

MARCUS AURELIUS, *MEDITATIONS*, 6.39

If you love those who love you, what credit is that to you? For even sinners love those who love them. If you do good to those who do good to you, what credit is that to you? For even sinners do the same. If you lend to those from whom you hope to receive, what credit is that to you? Even sinners lend to sinners, to receive back as much. But love your enemies, and do good, and lend, expecting nothing back; and your reward will be great, and you will be children of the Most High; for he is kind toward the unthankful and evil.

LUKE 6.32–35

So let every one of you, who is eager to be or to gain a friend, eradicate [faulty] judgments, hate them, drive them out of your mind. If you do that, then in the first place, you will never criticize yourself or be in conflict with yourself, and you will be free from inward reproach and self-torture; and, in the second place, in relation to other people, you will be always straightforward to every like-minded person, while to everyone who is unlike you, you will be tolerant, gentle, kindly, forgiving, as to one who is ignorant or is making a mistake in things of the greatest importance.

EPICTETUS, *DISCOURSES*, 2.22, 34–36

Greater love has no one than this, that
someone lay down his life for his friends.

John 15.13

For what purpose do I make a friend? In order to have someone for whom I may die, whom I may follow into exile, against whose death I may stake my own life.

SENECA, *MORAL LETTERS TO LUCILIUS*, 9.10

For if you love those who love you, what reward do you have? Don't even the tax collectors do the same? If you only greet your friends, what more do you do than others? Don't even the tax collectors do the same?

MATTHEW 5.46–47

Those who try to stand in your way when you act according to right reason will not be able to turn you aside from your proper action. Likewise, do not allow them to deter you from benevolent feelings, but be on your guard: not only in the matter of steady judgement and action, but also in the matter of gentleness towards those who try to hinder or otherwise trouble you. For it is also a weakness to be angry at them, as well as to be distracted from your course of action and give way through fear. Both have gone astray: the person who acts wrongly through fear, and the person who is alienated from those who are by nature kinfolk and friends.

MARCUS AURELIUS, *MEDITATIONS*, 11.9

This is my commandment, that you love one another, even as I have loved you.

John 15.12

Humans find contentment by doing what is most fitting for a human. And the most appropriate work of a human being is to be benevolent to other people.

MARCUS AURELIUS, *MEDITATIONS*, 8.26

INNER PEACE

Letting go: of the things that don't matter, of the things that aren't within your control, of the things that are not your responsibility. Jesus and the Stoics tell us this is the path to peace and a blessed life. Yet we need to be careful. This doesn't mean we sit around and do nothing. We must still take action, but with a mindset of aligning ourselves with God or the universe (whatever you believe). Letting go means releasing our own need to control what happens—or what we think should happen in a perfect world—and instead working dynamically and responsively with what is actually here in front of us.

For Christians, trusting in God's will is a matter of faith, of believing that God has your best interests at heart. For Stoics, aligning yourself with the cosmos is simply logical; as Seneca points out, "Do you consider it fairer that you should obey Nature, or that Nature should obey you?" In the same way, we can choose to let go and flow with the universe (or God's will), or we can strive against it, remaining angry and ineffective. Which route will you choose? Will you grasp and cling, or will you open yourself to loving acceptance? We may not always like what happens to us, but when we learn to accept and even welcome it, we are one step closer to inner peace.

Therefore, I tell you, don't be anxious for your life, what you will eat, nor yet for your body, what you will wear. Life is more than food, and the body is more than clothing.

LUKE 12.22–23

Some things are under our control, while others are not under our control. Under our control are opinion, choice, desire, aversion, and, in a word, everything that is our own doing; not under our control are our body, our property, reputation, position, and, in a word, everything that is not our own doing. The things under our control are by nature free, unhindered, and unimpeded; while the things not under our control are weak, servile, subject to hindrance, and not our own.

EPICTETUS, *HANDBOOK*, 1.1–2

Don't be anxious for tomorrow, for tomorrow will be anxious for itself. Each day's own trouble is enough.

MATTHEW 6.34

Do not let the future disturb you, for you will come to it, if necessary, bringing with you the same reason that you now use to deal with the present.

MARCUS AURELIUS, *MEDITATIONS*, 7.8

Which of you, by being anxious, can add a cubit to his height? If then you aren't able to do even the least things, why are you anxious about the rest?

LUKE 12.25–26

When I see a man in anxiety, I say to myself, "What can it be that he wants?" For if he did not want something that was outside of his control, how could he still remain in anxiety?

EPICTETUS, *DISCOURSES*, 2.13, 1

Peace I leave with you. My peace I give to you; not as the world gives, I give to you. Don't let your heart be troubled, neither let it be fearful.

John 14.27

When a person has this kind of peace proclaimed to him, not by Caesar—for how could *he* possibly proclaim it?—but proclaimed by God through reason, is he not content when he is alone? When he contemplates and reflects, "Now no evil can befall me, for me there is no such thing as a criminal, for me there is no such thing as an earthquake, everything is full of peace, everything full of tranquility; every road, every city, every fellow-traveler, neighbor, companion, all are harmless."

EPICTETUS, *DISCOURSES*, 3.13, 12–13

See the birds of the sky, that they don't sow, neither do they reap, nor gather into barns. Your heavenly Father feeds them. Aren't you of much more value than they? Which of you by being anxious, can add one moment to his lifespan?

MATTHEW 6.25–27

Does a good man fear that food will fail him? It does not fail the blind; it does not fail the lame; will it fail a good man? A good soldier, or workman, or cobbler does not lack someone to give him pay; and so should a good man? Does God so neglect his own creatures, his servants, his witnesses, whom alone he uses as examples to the uninstructed, to prove that he exists and governs the universe well, and does not neglect the affairs of men, and that no evil befalls a good man either in life or in death?

EPICTETUS, *DISCOURSES*, 3.26, 27–28

WALKING THE PATH

The path is never easy. Finding the path, walking the path, knowing (or not knowing) where the path will lead you—these are the great challenges of each person's life. Some people never even look for it. Some people don't think it exists. But seekers from the beginning of time have known it was there, and these seekers have left us a map to follow.

Jesus famously told his followers, "I am the way, the truth, and the life. No one comes to the Father, except through me" (John 14.6). But what exactly does he mean by this? In *Reading the Bible Again for the First Time*, Marcus Borg suggests that Jesus is giving instructions about leaving the selfish concerns of the world behind, asking us to shed our old way of being and enter into a new life. But this path is not exclusive to Christianity. It is a universal path known to all the great wisdom traditions:

I think that following this internal path is pretty much necessary for every human being. The foundation for what I'm saying is that the growing-up process, what we call the process of socialization, involves internalizing the messages of our elders and of our culture—messages about what's worth pursuing in life, about what we should look like, about what being successful means, and so forth. And so we intrinsically end up living under the tyranny of all of these voices that are telling us what to do . . .

Because our socialization intrinsically leads to that kind of self-preoccupation, with how well the self is doing, the path of release and liberation from that self-preoccupation intrinsically involves dying to that way of being and being born to a life that is centered in the spirit, or in what William James in his wonderfully generic term for God called "the more." To be centered in "the more" and not in the standards of my culture, not in the standards of my religious tradition, not in myself and how "well" I'm doing. To use Christian language once again, the primary fruit of centering in "the more," according to St. Paul, are the four gifts of the spirit: peace, joy, freedom, and love. Now, who wouldn't want a life filled with those things? And I see those fruits of the spirit to be the fruits of the spiritual life, in all

> of the major religious traditions. I don't see this as peculiar to Christianity. I see Christianity as the revelation of a universal path, rather than its being the revelation or disclosure of a unique path.[28]

Obviously, this path, as described by Borg, is also the Stoic path: changing our values from external to internal, leaving behind our old habits and embarking on a new way of life, fully committing ourselves to practices and actions that prioritize virtue and goodwill. When we do so, we will enjoy "peace, joy, freedom, and love," or as the Greeks called it, *eudaimonia*.

Like Marcus Borg, the ancient Stoics believed we are socialized in unhealthy ways. If we remain stuck in the dominant values of our society, we will never find happiness or fulfillment. Our emancipation lies in rejecting the egotistical concerns of the world, including wealth, status, and power, but also our need to be right, or to prove ourselves better than other people, or to be important and admired. Walking the path means looking past false appearances, devoting ourselves to truth and goodness, filling our hearts and minds with love, letting go of those things we can't control—in other words, everything we have studied in this book.

Thank you for walking this path together with me. Though the way is difficult, the terrain rough, and the outcome at times uncertain, we are certainly not alone.

We walk alongside all those who (to borrow William James's term) have sought "the more" in life. Perhaps you feel Jesus walking with you, carrying you through the difficult times, guiding you toward your ultimate destination. Perhaps you rely instead on role models like Socrates, Epictetus, and Marcus Aurelius to show you the way to *eudaimonia*. Or perhaps both. But whatever your persuasion, I hope this book has been a helpful signpost on your path to the good life. I wish you much joy, peace, and love in your journey with Jesus and the Stoics.

Enter in by the narrow gate; for the gate is wide and the way is broad that leads to destruction, and there are many who enter in by it. How narrow is the gate and the way is restricted that leads to life! There are few who find it.

Matthew 7.13–14

You can pass your life in a constant state
of happiness if you walk the right path,
and think and act in the right way.

MARCUS AURELIUS, *MEDITATIONS*, 5.34

Everyone who hears these words of mine and does them, I will liken him to a wise man who built his house on the rock. The rain came down, the floods came, and the winds blew and beat on that house; and it didn't fall, for it was founded on the rock. Everyone who hears these words of mine and doesn't do them will be like a foolish man who built his house on the sand. The rain came down, the floods came, and the winds blew and beat on that house; and it fell—and its fall was great.

Matthew 7.24–27

Will you not lay this foundation to begin with—that is, examine your decision and see whether it is sound or unsound, and then afterwards build on it your firmness and unshaken resolve? But if you lay a rotten and crumbling foundation, you will not be able to build even a tiny building; the bigger and stronger the edifice that you build on it, the quicker it will collapse.

EPICTETUS, *DISCOURSES*, 2.15, 8–9

He also told a parable to them. "No one puts a piece from a new garment on an old garment, or else he will tear the new, and also the piece from the new will not match the old. No one puts new wine into old wineskins, or else the new wine will burst the skins, and it will be spilled and the skins will be destroyed. But new wine must be put into fresh wineskins, and both are preserved. No man having drunk old wine immediately desires new, for he says, 'The old is better.'"

LUKE 5.36–39

Choose, then, which you prefer—to be like your former self and be loved as before by those who loved you, or to be better than before, and so miss what they once gave you. For if this is the better choice, then incline to this, and let no other considerations draw you away, for no one can make progress by facing both ways. But if you have chosen this course above all others, if you wish to devote yourself to this and nothing else, and to spend all your labor on this, then dismiss all other thoughts, or else this facing both ways will produce a double result—you will not make progress as you ought, and you will fail to get what you got before.

EPICTETUS, *DISCOURSES*, 4.2, 3–5

Jesus answered, "Aren't there twelve hours of daylight? If a man walks in the day, he doesn't stumble, because he sees the light of this world. But if a man walks in the night, he stumbles, because the light isn't in him."

JOHN 11.9–10

The light may begin to shine if we are willing. But such a result can only happen in one way—if we acquire knowledge of things divine and human.

SENECA, *MORAL LETTERS TO LUCILIUS*, 110.8

He was reclining at the table in his house, and many tax collectors and sinners sat down with Jesus and his disciples, for there were many, and they followed him. The scribes and the Pharisees, when they saw that he was eating with the sinners and tax collectors, said to his disciples, "Why is it that he eats and drinks with tax collectors and sinners?"

When Jesus heard it, he said to them, "Those who are healthy have no need for a physician, but those who are sick. I came not to call the righteous, but sinners to repentance."

MARK 2.15–17

The philosopher's school is a hospital; you shouldn't walk out of it in pleasure, but in pain. For you are not well when you come; one man has a dislocated shoulder, another an abscess, another a fistula, another a headache. And then you would have me sit there and utter fine little thoughts and phrases, so you may leave me with praise on your lips—one man carrying away his shoulder just as it was when he came in, another his head in the same state, another his fistula, another his abscess?

EPICTETUS, *DISCOURSES*, 3.23, 30-31

On that day, Jesus went out of the house and sat by the seaside. Great multitudes gathered to him, so that he entered into a boat and sat; and all the multitude stood on the beach. He spoke to them many things in parables, saying, "Behold, a farmer went out to sow. As he sowed, some seeds fell by the roadside, and the birds came and devoured them. Others fell on rocky ground, where they didn't have much soil, and immediately they sprang up, because they had no depth of earth. When the sun had risen, they were scorched. Because they had no root, they withered away. Others fell among thorns. The thorns grew up and choked them. Others fell on good soil and yielded fruit: some one hundred times as much, some sixty, and some thirty. He who has ears to hear, let him hear."

MATTHEW 13.1–9

Now you are a poor plant of this kind. You have blossomed too soon; the winter will kill you. Look what farmers say about seeds when the hot weather comes before its time. They are all anxiety for fear that the seeds should grow insolent and then a single frost seize them and expose their weakness. You, too, man, must beware: you have grown insolent and have leapt to an opinion before the time: you think yourself a somebody, fool that you are among fools; you will be frost-bitten—no, you are already frost-bitten down at the root, though above you still blossom for a while and therefore think you are still alive and flourishing. Leave us at least to ripen as nature wishes.

EPICTETUS, *DISCOURSES*, 4.8, 37–40

He set another parable before them, saying, "The Kingdom of Heaven is like a grain of mustard seed which a man took, and sowed in his field, which indeed is smaller than all seeds. But when it is grown, it is greater than the herbs and becomes a tree, so that the birds of the air come and lodge in its branches."

MATTHEW 13.31–32

Words should be scattered like seed; no matter how small the seed may be, once it has found favorable ground, it unfolds its strength and from an insignificant thing spreads to its greatest growth. Reason grows in the same way; it does not appear large but increases as it does its work. Few words are spoken, but if the mind has truly caught them, they grow strong and spring up. Yes, precepts and seeds have the same quality; they are slight things, but they produce much.

SENECA, *MORAL LETTERS TO LUCILIUS*, 38.2

Most certainly I tell you, unless one is born of water and Spirit, he can't enter into God's Kingdom. That which is born of the flesh is flesh. That which is born of the Spirit is spirit. Don't marvel that I said to you, "You must be born anew."

JOHN 3.5–7

As there are these two elements united in our composition, the body which we share with the animals, and the reason and mind which we share with the gods, some of us incline toward the former relationship, which is unblessed by fortune and is mortal, and only a few toward that which is divine and blessed.

EPICTETUS, *DISCOURSES*, 1.3, 3

Jesus spoke to them, saying, "I am the light of the world. He who follows me will not walk in the darkness, but will have the light of life."

JOHN 8.12

Someday the secrets of nature will be disclosed to you, the haze will be shaken from your eyes, and the bright light will stream in upon you from all sides . . . Then you will realize you have lived in darkness, after you have seen, in your perfect state, the perfect light—that light which you now barely see with vision that is impaired to the greatest degree. Even now, far off as it is, you already look at it in wonder; what do you think the heavenly light will be when you have truly seen it?

SENECA, *MORAL LETTERS TO LUCILIUS*, 102.28

Jesus therefore said to those Jews who had believed him, "If you remain in my word, then you are truly my disciples. You will know the truth, and the truth will make you free."

JOHN 8.31–32

What is the happy life? It is peace of mind and lasting tranquility. This will be yours if you possess greatness of soul; it will be yours if you possess the steadfastness that resolutely clings to good judgment. How do you reach this condition? By gaining a complete view of truth, by maintaining, in all that you do, order, measure, decency, and a will that is friendly and generous, that is intent upon reason and never departs from it, that commands at the same time love and admiration. In short, the wise person's soul would be fitting for a god.

SENECA, *MORAL LETTERS TO LUCILIUS*, 92.3

ENDNOTES

1 Marcus Borg, ed., *Jesus and Buddha: The Parallel Sayings* (Ulysses Press, 1997), 25.
2 Niko Huttunen, "Stoic Law in Paul?" in *Stoicism in Early Christianity*, ed. Tuomas Rasimus, Troels Engberg-Pedersen, and Ismo Dunderberg (Baker Academic, 2010).
3 Troels Engberg-Pedersen, "Setting the Scene: Stoicism and Platonism in the Transitional Period in Ancient Philosophy," in *Stoicism in Early Christianity*, ed. Tuomas Rasimus, Troels Engberg-Pedersen, and Ismo Dunderberg (Baker Academic, 2010).
4 A. A. Long, *Epictetus: A Stoic and Socratic Guide to Life* (Oxford University Press, 2002), 259.
5 Elizabeth Agnew Cochran, "Stoicism and Christian Ethics," *St. Andrews Encyclopaedia of Theology*, 2022.
6 Elizabeth Agnew Cochran, *Protestant Virtue and Stoic Ethics* (Bloomsbury T&T Clark, 2017).
7 Kevin Vost, *The Porch and the Cross: Ancient Stoic Wisdom for Modern Christian Living* (Angelico Press, 2016), 14.
8 Borg, ed., *Jesus and Buddha*, 24.
9 Elaine Pagels, *Miracles and Wonder: The Historical Mystery of Jesus* (Doubleday, 2025), 116.
10 John Piper, *"Love Your Enemies": Jesus' Love Command in the Synoptic Gospels and the Early Christian Paranesis* (Cambridge University Press, 1980), 20.
11 Marcus Borg, *Reading the Bible Again for the First Time: Taking the Bible Seriously but Not Literally* (HarperSanFrancisco, 2001), 215.
12 Runar M. Thorsteinsson, "Stoicism as a Key to Pauline Ethics in Romans," in *Stoicism in Early Christianity*, ed. Tuomas Rasimus, Troels Engberg-Pedersen, and Ismo Dunderberg (Baker Academic, 2010), 34.

13 See Troels Engberg-Pedersen, *Paul and the Stoics* (Westminster John Knox Press, 2000); and Niko Huttunen, "Stoic Law in Paul?" in *Stoicism in Early Christianity*, ed. Tuomas Rasimus, Troels Engberg-Pedersen, and Ismo Dunderberg (Baker Academic, 2010).
14 Gitte Buch-Hansen, *"It is the Spirit that Gives Life": A Stoic Understanding of Pneuma in John's Gospel* (Walter De Gruyter, 2010); and Troels Engberg-Pedersen, *John and Philosophy: A New Reading of the Fourth Gospel* (Oxford University Press, 2017).
15 Stanley K. Stowers, "Jesus the Teacher and Stoic Ethics in the Gospel of Matthew," in *Stoicism in Early Christianity*, ed. Tuomas Rasimus, Troels Engberg-Pedersen, and Ismo Dunderberg (Baker Academic, 2010), 59.
16 Pierre Hadot, *Qu'est-ce que la philosophie antique?*, (Éditions Gallimard, 1995), 355–356.
17 Runar M. Thorsteinsson, *Roman Christianity and Roman Stoicism: A Comparative Study of Ancient Morality* (Oxford University Press, 2010), 209.
18 Karen Armstrong, *The Great Transformation: The Beginning of Our Religious Traditions* (Alfred A. Knopf, 2006).
19 Armstrong, *The Great Transformation*, 571.
20 Armstrong, *The Great Transformation*, 8.
21 Borg, ed., *Jesus and Buddha*, 17.
22 Pierre Hadot, "Conversion," in *Exercises Spirituels et Philosophie Antique* (Albin Michel, 2002), 226.
23 Hadot, "Conversion," in *Exercises Spirituels et Philosophie Antique*, 226.
24 Borg, *Reading the Bible Again for the First Time*, 327.
25 Borg, ed., *Jesus and Buddha*, 25.
26 Stanley K. Stowers, "Jesus the Teacher and Stoic Ethics in the Gospel of Matthew," in *Stoicism in Early Christianity*, ed. Tuomas Rasimus, Troels Engberg-Pedersen, and Ismo Dunderberg (Baker Academic, 2010), p. 68.
27 For more details on Stoic technical concepts, see *Stoic Ethics: The Basics* by Christopher Gill and Brittany Polat (Routledge, 2024).
28 Borg, *Reading the Bible Again for the First Time*, 340.

BIBLIOGRAPHY

Epictetus. *The Discourses and Manual, Together with Fragments of His Writings*. Translated by P. E. Matheson. Clarendon Press, 1916.

Epictetus. *Discourses, Books 1–2*. Translated by W. A. Oldfather. Harvard University Press, 1925.

Epictetus. *Discourses, Books 3–4. Fragments. The Encheiridion*. Translated by W. A. Oldfather. Harvard University Press, 1928.

Epictetus. *The Discourses of Epictetus, with the Encheiridion and Fragments*. Translated by George Long. George Bell and Sons, 1890.

Marcus Aurelius. *Meditations of Marcus Aurelius*. Translated by George Long. Blackie and Son, 1910.

Musonius Rufus. "Musonius Rufus 'The Roman Socrates.'" Translated by Cora Lutz. In *Yale Classical Studies*, vol. 10. Yale University Press, 1947.

Seneca. *Ad Lucilium Epistulae Morales*, Vol 1. Translated by Richard M. Gummere. William Heinemann, 1917.

Seneca. *Ad Lucilium Epistulae Morales*, Vol. 2. Translated by Richard M. Gummere. William Heinemann, 1920.

Seneca. *Ad Lucilium Epistulae Morales*, Vol. 3. Translated by Richard M. Gummere. William Heinemann, 1925.

Seneca. *Minor Dialogues, Together with the Dialogue on Clemency*. Translated by Aubrey Stewart. George Bell and Sons, 1889.

Seneca. *On Benefits*. Translated by Aubrey Stewart. George Bell and Sons, 1887.

ACKNOWLEDGMENTS

My sincere thanks to Claire Sielaff, my editor at Ulysses, who initiated this project and who was a delight to work with; and to Chris Gill, for insightful comments on this manuscript and enduring good advice.

ABOUT THE AUTHOR

Brittany Polat is a philosophical writer and community organizer who shares Stoicism with people all over the world. Her previous books include *Stoic Ethics: The Basics* (with Christopher Gill) and *Journal Like a Stoic*. Find more of her work on Substack at Stoicism for Humans, or join her for Stoic community events through Modern Stoicism or Stoicare.